T0367963

MAY BE
HABIT
FORMING

MAY BE HABIT FORMING

MICHELLE MOUSA

ARCHWAY
PUBLISHING

"You are the bows from which your children

as living arrows are sent forth."

The Prophet Khalil Gibran

"Come on now, it's freedom calling

Come on over and find yourself"

Foreigner Suite, Cat Stevens

To my mom and dad for everything

To my Amelia Bedelia, Annie

To my children, Tara, Aimee and Rocky,

my heart and soul here on Earth

Archway Publishing books may be ordered through booksellers or by contacting:

Archway Publishing
1663 Liberty Drive
Bloomington, IN 47403
www.archwaypublishing.com
844-669-3957

ISBN: 978-1-6657-6090-4 (sc)
ISBN: 978-1-6657-6091-1 (e)

Library of Congress Control Number: 2024910958

Print information available on the last page.

Archway Publishing rev. date: 06/13/2024

Mutual of Omaha

Sunday afternoons

Wild Kingdom

Marlin Perkins

Wildlife adventures

Watching the lions pounce

Safari adventure from our wingback chairs

Always next to daddy

Waiting for the next prey

Always waiting

California

Flying to California

so excited

can't sleep

The city looks like Christmas time

bright lights all around

Houses stacked

one by one

nothing flat

first stop to cousins I've never met

Dinosaur mountain

up ahead

always sleeping

Millbrae

my new city

my new home

my new room

Cul- de- sac

palm trees

featured in a magazine

Fifth grade

mom walked me in

tried to make a friend

so uncomfortable

embarrassed

All the eyes looking back at me

Dorothy in The Wizard of Oz

I sing "Somewhere Over The Rainbow'

I'm so proud my family is there

I hope they are proud of me

Edelweiss

I want to be an actress

Nun in Sound of Music

In love with Captain von Trapp

Swoon

6th Grade Crush

Everyone downstairs except for three of us

High School Cast Party

What a loser I am

I felt it that day for the first time

I brought the music

But nobody wanted to dance with me

A Nun in the "Sound of Music"

Tilly in "He who Gets Slapped"

A Virgin and a Fat Clown

Both parts of me

Company

Peaches, plums and pears,

grapes, cantaloupe, honeydew

all the fruit

get it out

wash it

cut it

put it on the platter

Company

They'll be here soon

serve serve serve

no thank you no thank you no thank you

OK I'll have some

might as well

clear plates

wash the dishes

put away

until next time

Westland Mall

Taxi please!

Time to get out of the house

Run to the alabaster dinosaur statue and egg

Or is it a goose

Climbing, and climbing

Mama and my sisters

Saturday afternoon shopping

Nowhere to be

Having fun

Not afraid

No stranger danger yet

Etch a sketch on a desk

Am I really lost?

Do they really miss me?

Westland Mall on a Saturday

It takes care of all of us

Up the Street

Up the street I go

Can't wait to get there

An apartment and a pool

Her mom works long hours

The whole place to ourselves

Tom Petty

Don't have to be a Refugee

But want to be

Not my house

Not my mom

Doing the things that I get to do

Nobody watching me

Nobody telling me to stop

Runaway up the street

Runaway from all the rules

Run away from my life

Run away from me

Piano Lessons

It makes her happy

I want to make her happy

The teacher smells like cinnamon

Grab the lesson sheets from in the bench

I want to smash the lid on my fingers

Dementia

Bacon

Ledges

Living on the edge

Big flower bag to put things in

I am beautiful

No more about my hair or my tired eyes

Flowers cover the calendar

This is Liz's room and we are eating her food

Leftover salad tastes good

Sit down get comfortable

Play war

Some people play cards by themselves, but I never did

This is Mom

Room 221 Bed B

A clock

A TV

A Dresser

A Wheelchair

A Walker

A closet of clothes

Pictures

Lotions

Gold bracelets

Water cup from Wynn Casino

Dark Chocolate Almonds

Pumpkin seeds

Round Bread

Nurse Julia lunchbox

Cafeteria, smelling of ketchup

Hard to open

Don't want to open

Kids sitting near me

Not too close

Round bread coming out

Half in, half out

Bending down to take a bite

Jelly oozing out the bottom

Yummy – taste so good

Don't want round bread at school

At home with zait and zaatar

At home with rice and meat

At home with hummus

No round bread at school

Please

Binti

It means daughter

But more

It means she is mine

She is my girl

I'm bint Shawky

I am my father's daughter

It's a very special word like Dar Meen?

What house, what family are you from

More important than your name

A placeholder

It lets others know who you come from

Who you are of

Not the mom, only the dad

Five girls- I'm the last one

No sons

Poor dad

He called me Mish Mish

His little apricot

I wish I was a boy

I always wished that for him

Daddy told me once he was glad he only had girls

"If I had a boy, I would've killed him" he said

I believed him at the time

I don't think he meant it

I guess it's best he had just girls

I am Jannette's daughter, too

Bint Jannette and Shawky

My Tata

Every three months

My bedroom became her bedroom

Her long gray hair twisted up

Her and my mom in the kitchen

Her black purse

"Jibbi juzdani"

"Bring me my purse"

Washing her back on Sundays

back-and-forth back-and-forth

using a loofah sponge

my grandmother, my Tata

going from house to house

displaced

so many sons and so many daughters

No more home and no more country

Three Drinks

Harrah's Casino

Harvey's

Summit Room's escargot

Three drink minimum

Big U shaped Booths facing the stage

VIP treatment

Front of the line

Bob Newhart

Dyan Cannon

Teddy Pendergrass

Pit bosses

Baccarat behind closed doors

the bells

the jackpots

the smoke

the chips

the wheel

the roulette

the poker

Only blackjack for me

third base seat

don't need to eat

don't need to sleep

always breaking even

Hit me

Two Babies

The doctor said there are two

I didn't believe it

I started laughing, uncontrollable laughter

How could this be?

I wasn't even ready for one

we're going to have two?

God is so funny

Hilarious

Driving to my parent's house

Can't wait to tell them

so excited, so scared

TWINS

Maybe a boy and a girl

Instant family

That would be nice

Feels like cheating

How lucky are we?

Two babies

Do they run in the family?

When did you find out?

It's going to be a boy and a girl

We will name them

Rocky and Jannette

Instant Family

Teri Drive

Goldfish flopping
flip-flopping on the basement stair
backyard sprinkler in summertime
ice cream truck singing by

My cousin just down the street
the smell of Makloubeh
mama's making for dinner

Running in the kitchen
sneaking a few
roasted cauliflower pieces from the
counter cooling on the pan

Where are you Ramallah?

Hard-working families

one town

mom and dad pushed out

left home to a strange land

the Nakba, the Catastrophe

immigrant fathers and mothers

This place I've never been

this place I almost saw

grinding wheat, cultivating groves

gardens of grapes, and olives

planting, always planting

cows, sheep, goats, donkeys and horses

The old men play backgammon- towla

the women breaking the olives- zatoon

the children running in the fields

a place a father came to with his young daughter long ago

running running

Where are you Ramallah?

beautiful city I heard about my whole life

the theater

the ice cream place

the beautiful hills

the beautiful people

the beautiful city

Where are you Ramallah?

my mom and dad's town

their home

their land

The song was always playing

Saweh

I ache for you Ramallah

I hope to meet you someday

Serenity Knolls

Sitting in the intake office
signing my name
never been so scared and defeated
sick and tired of being sick and tired
sick BAY
Jerry Garcia died here

I'm broken detoxing and defeated
I'm still thinking about famous people
get up and get coffee Michelle
that's what Barbara said
no one serving it to me here
arrogant and self-righteous
Down to the Hill house?
doesn't make sense
walking into that dining hall defeated
hearing the laughter
seeing people smiling

Get the cream for my coffee

None of that powdered shit

"Relax- God is in Charge" written on

the magnet on the fridge

I take my first deep breath

34 years old

God I don't want to be here, but there's no place else to go

my children need me

I need them

I think I'll stay

Precious

I wanted to jump in

To catch a glimpse of what could be

Never have I ever clearly understood

A love so bright

A love so free

Why for me?

Why not for me?

Take it in

Precious is what she called me

Anxiety

Perfection

If I can accept myself as she accepts me

Eternal quiet

No more voices of my little girl

You keep leaving me

Why won't you pay attention to me

I give my life over to the joy

Like Lucy from Charlie Brown

Nothing Bad

Little one

Scared of so many things

Frightened

Night terrors

Banging your head to fall asleep

"He's self soothing," the doctor said

I want to soothe you my little boy

Nothing bad tonight or any night was the promise I made

Night time once again

Sleep came slowly for you little one

Help you get through one more night

Distractions soothed you

and

Wizard of Oz

Ninja Turtles

Transformers

Baseball Cards

Slot Cars

Magic

No more little boy

No more night terrors

Children of your own

All is well

It is what it is

Good Mom

Keeping track

Feeding them

Taking walks

Sun is good for them

Bath every night

Clean babies

Good Mom

Music class

Gymboree

Mommy and Me and Me

Twins club

Matching outfits

Good Mom

Sharing

Snacks

Shoes that fit

Watching them carefully

Sandbox

Singing to them

Learning nursery rhymes

Dots n Dashes haircuts

Good Mom

Sick babies

Doctors office visits

Birthday parties

Trips to zoo

Smiles and Laughter

Crying and Screaming

Please stop

Let's go home

Good Mom

May Be Habit Forming

Open houses

I told them to check out the bedrooms

Go see who would sleep where!

The realtor greeted me in the kitchen

Asked me to sign the guest book

Never my name

Was I interested in the house?

I had my answer ready

"I live close by"

"I was just looking at it for remodeling ideas"

I walked around downstairs and

waited until she started looking at her phone

Time to get upstairs

Not much time before she follows me

Straight to the master bathroom

That's where they always were

The medicine cabinet

No time

I hear the kids

Grab them all

No time to look

I'll look at them later

Kids in the car

Realtor comes out of house and stares

I feel the stare

The kids were rambling

Talking about so many different things

What they saw

who would sleep where

My heart was pounding

thinking about what treasures I had in my purse

I could not function without them

Everyday

Counting always counting

Need more for tomorrow

I've lost the ability to do my day without them

May be habit forming

Every bottle said that

I thought that didn't apply to me

Because It Came From You

I'm feeling melancholy

Shadows

Laughter

Tears

Stumbling around the dark

No one home

Something familiar

Don't wait up

I have somewhere to be

I can't tell you more than that

We helped ourselves and put the rest away

Don't worry about the dishes

I'll take care of them when I return

Foreigner

Where did she belong

If she didn't belong here?

She always wanted to be Irish

Nobody had problems with Irish people so she thought

After the PLO bombing

during the Olympics

her mom was so scared

She used to say she was Greek

or Lebanese

or Egyptian

Anything but Palestinian

Her dad's beautiful name

Shawky

named after a poet his mother heard

while pregnant with him

He became Chuck

to the grocery workers and delivery men

Easier to pronounce, he said

She thought it was safer that way

safer for him and for his family

She loves the Arabic language

but doesn't want us to speak it in public

She hears others speak it on television and in the movies

She gets a smile on her face

It feels like home

Spring Valley

She walked into the classroom

She saw her teacher

She knew that it would be a good day

Her desk

Her pencils

Glue sticks, erasers, binder paper

lesson of the day- a quick write

Multi use room 11:15

Fear and panic

She didn't like being in the crowd

She wasn't sure why

all those kids made her breathe funny

She didn't like recess

she would hide in the alcove

between the two bathrooms

and read her book

She didn't like lunch

with the round bread

that she always had in her lunchbox

Never knowing where to sit

She didn't like PE

Having to wear the too small blue cotton uniform

with front snaps that always unsnapped

Bust too big

Finally back to class

To her desk

Her island

With her teacher

She can breathe again

Buildings

Buildings

liquor stores everywhere

Harrison Street

people walking with their dogs

Buildings

cars lined up like dominos

insomnia

Buildings

homeless

buses

cable cars

Buildings

trash

can't turn right

can't turn left

one way only

bars and liquor stores everywhere

Buildings

overpasses

motorcycles

billboards on ramps off ramps

wrong way

Drumstick Thighs

Twelve years old

overweight

Millbrae Rec Center

Dropped off at Weight Watchers

hiding cereal in my room

cookies and milk

so much loneliness

"Drumstick thighs" he joked

Stopped eating the whole week

Church camp

so proud of myself for not eating

forced to drink milk

poured down my mouth

eating disorder

anorexic

bulimic

Do I have an eating disorder?

I like food way too much

like the comfort of it

Fosters Freeze with the cone and dipped in chocolate

so excited

With daddy

the wall at the side of the building

Birds nest in the hole

Tiny, not like me

The Basement

Growing up

there was a basement floor

braided rug

the big sofa

best of all

wooden console TV

Mike Douglas

Dinah Shore

Phil Donahue

Days of our Lives

One Life to Live

All I needed to know

loved the basement

twirling around the black pole

my hands raw

getting dizzy

my first high I remember

my colored hat

stripes of rainbow colors

I would wear it like a magic cap

No noise

just me and the television

I loved the weekly TV guide

circling what I was going to watch every half hour

my day was planned

on school days I would rush home

put my pajamas on

in the afternoon

Sun was out

run downstairs to the dark basement

my circus and my carnival

Needy

want to be something other than what I am

you make it look so easy

Need to be liked

Need to be included

left outness I used to call it

I thought it was because I was the youngest

The baby

maybe not

Need to be seen

Need to be heard

Lots of needs

As I grow older

I feel filled up

I feel heard

I feel a part of

The Elevator

She said I could come in

She was planting in her backyard

Her daughter's birthday party was tomorrow

She told me the elevator was going down

I could stay on or I could get off

May 31, 1996

My last day of being drunk,being high

I was so scared

I knew the solution

I just didn't know if I could do it

The faces of my children

The promise of a new life

The small room

at the back of the bookstore

would be the beginning

1994

It was such a headache

I'll just take one

phone calls to make before getting off of work

need to leave and pick up the kids

A feeling of ease and comfort came over me

washed over me

never knew what euphoria was

until that moment

Didn't even know to call it that

Made dinner

Homework

Baths

Bedtime

Couldn't wait to go back to work the next morning

I thought about it on the drive there

I did not have a headache

I wasn't in any pain

but I wanted that relief

I went in the medicine room

samples in the cardboard box

Not locked up yet

No one knew yet how dangerous they were

Two to a pack

little white foil

Grabbed ten of them

put them in my pockets of my uniform

went to the bathroom

was so excited

ripped open the foil pack

popped them both

came out of the bathroom

and quickly downed them with some coffee

Called in the next patient

and waited joyfully for that feeling

oh my God it came so quickly

how had I lived this long without them

32 years old

Little white pills

Vicodin

hydrocodone

May Be Habit Forming

1995

Baths every day

I wanted to take a bath every day to soak

People magazines

Danielle Steele books

my kids in the other room

I'm unavailable

Leave me alone

Go do your homework

watch TV

I'll be out in a little bit

close my door

get the hell out!

I didn't care about anything

or anyone

Gone were the days when I could calm their fears

I was sick

I was really sick

I couldn't eat

I couldn't sleep

Driving recklessly for prescriptions

yelling, and screaming and slapping

washed over me when I took the pills again

I didn't care

it was heaven and hell

the arrest

the running

plowing down mailbox

Housewife

flowers in the spring

pumpkins in the fall

Christmas trees in winter

Family portrait

all in denim by the white gazebo

Burdens

I cannot take from you

what you won't release

to me higher power is here for me

Where am I?

I look inward and all I see is the shame

I've heard it

God Laughs at our plans

If I truly live in this moment

I know that God's got me

why is this way so hard for me

an open heart not a closed one

A body for healing not for hurting

Letter to Vicodin

Dear Vicodin,

when we first met,

I was working in Walnut Creek

and feeling stressed

I started to use you and just take a

few of you home with me

for the afternoon

I found that you made my life easier to handle

and you made my energy level so much better

I felt great when I left work to spend

more time with the kids

and to get away from the drugs, but

I began to miss you a lot

I was in conflict

Knew I shouldn't be taking you

knew I was now abusing you,

I still wanted you

I plunged into my illegal behavior

phoning and forging prescriptions

to bring you home

I lived for you and when I could get more of you

Always counting and running out of you

money spent on you

Arrested

leaving the kids at home to score

God loves me and forgives me but God

help me get through this too.

Goodbye Vicodin,

Michelle

Famous

Movie Theaters

Plays

Books

Television

Clark Gable Poster in my room

Katherine and Marilyn Books read over and over.

Hometown stages

Broadway stages

drama major for a minute

I wanna be in the movies

I wanna write a book

Do I matter if I'm not famous

I'll pay the price

sign me up

Therapy

I'm told I need therapy

I'm overwhelmed

Get through the day

Something's wrong

Try to be happy

I should be happy

Prozac 20 mg once a day

He said it would help

drinking helped

taking pills helped

Go to therapy

Identified patient

Roles we play

you're sick

you need to be better

Somethings wrong with you

Look at all you have

why can't you just be happy

Go to therapy

get better

change your thinking

change your mind

Change your ways

Change your habits

change everything about you

Change how you feel

Do better

get better

Be better

Go to therapy

Talk about how you feel

tell the truth

In the Middle

Always wanting to get my way

Never wanting to compromise

Always feeling that I was right

Never wanted to be wrong

Always trying to win

Never wanting to lose

Always trying to catch up

Never wanting to be behind

Always wanting to be a part of

Never wanted to be left out

always

never

always

never

now it doesn't matter

Always and never are both losing

time to just be in the middle

Maybe

we'll see

sounds good

Let me think about it

Say more about that

So much happier when I'm in the middle.

Room 711

My dad said he was in room 711

I knew that he would be OK

That's a lucky number

Especially for a gambler

He said I don't think so

Not this time

I didn't want to see him in the hospital

one more time

I said I'll come see him when he is better

I got a call from my niece

My dad was dead

March 4

I like that date

Marching forth into heaven

so grateful he was out of pain

out of misery

out of all the discomfort

Dad built a home here in America

for his wife and his daughters

I try not to feel too sad for him

he always used to sit in the garage

smoked his cigarettes

read his newspaper

Mom didn't want him smoking in the house

There really wasn't a place for him

At least that's what makes me sad

Bonnie and Clyde

I knew it as soon as I saw him on his phone

looking right at me

I still walked up to the counter

because I needed them

leaving wasn't an option

my name my name, oh right

What was the name for this pharmacy

My little burgundy book had all my false names

A different one for each pharmacy

Susan

the pharmacist came from behind the counter

started talking to me

asking me what I took the pain medicine for

He was stalling

cops were coming

It was May 12, 1996

Aimee and Tara's birthday party was that afternoon

What an idiot I was

trying to forge prescriptions on my daughters' birthday

I didn't plan that very well.

"I have to go.

I forgot it's my daughters' birthday.

I need to get the cake".

I started to walk quickly out of the store.

I ran to my car, pulled out

and started to drive towards California Boulevard

A cop car swerved around right in front of me

My heart fell to my stomach

I've been arrested before, but not like this

Bonnie and Clyde shit

The cop escorted me to the corner of the parking lot

I got out

He got out

He grabbed my arm and had me sit on a cement block

right at the corner of two very busy streets

Demoralizing to say the least.

He handcuffed me

asked me if I knew why I was being arrested.

No

He asked me to state my name

Hmmmm

Do I give my real name?

Do I give the false name I just used?

I went with my real name

Why was I picking up a prescription for Susan?

I said she was a friend of mine.

"Why is there a problem?"

The lies just kept rolling out of my mouth.

It would be two more weeks before I was finally done

My Children's Children

How could I have known the wonder of being a grandma?

A Tata? A Tati?

Being a mother felt like a daily hustle of taking care of kids

nourishing them, keeping them clean, getting them to

school, signing them up for stuff. All year long.

How are you feeling?

What do you need?

Being someone's grandma is a whole different experience

The smiles and giggles

The special moments with each one

whispers into an ear

going to put mustard on you

hugs and kisses

gentle hand on my shoulder

reading together

shaving cream in the bath

water balloons

frozen yogurt

the library on Wednesdays

playlist made for each one

soothing

dependable

needed

Collectibles

Figurines placed

Lladros, Hummels, Royal Doultons

house to house

Curio cabinets

keep them clean and shiny

Names on the bottom

special items

How many do you have?

collectibles

give them away

Keep them

special items in the cabinet

always there to look at and admire.

Walkman

I put the borrowed Walkman on at the rehab

It was the day that music came back to me

So long since I could hear

Head full of lies

Losing My Religion by R.E.M.

I felt a calm come over me

And a sense of comfort

I looked out at Mount Tam

Life was going to be different now

Life is going to be bigger

Starter House

Walking in

I was a grown-up now

beautiful cul-de-sac

Nice big backyard trees

We would start a family here

House Arrest

It was a Wednesday when the parole officer put it on

I remember thinking how tight it was on my ankle

He told me the only thing I could do was attend

one 12 step meeting a day

add 30 minutes to and from

Point A to Point B and back again

I couldn't pick up my kids from school

I couldn't take them

I couldn't get groceries for our home

I had lost the privilege

The hard part was going to be telling the kids

there was no way around hiding the fact that their mom

did some bad things and she was being punished for it

He told me the deal

A black box with a phone on it was installed

in my room on my nightstand

It could ring at any time, day or night

I had to answer it by the third ring

no matter where I was in the house

I could be very far from the phone

they would ask random questions

I would not be able to answer them if I was high or drunk

The middle two numbers of your Social Security number

the year you were born backwards

the house number of your address

They ran with me to answer

There was a wand that you attached to the anklet

the random questions started

Their little faces looking at me

we were all on house arrest

Right On Time

When I taught 6th Grade Language Arts
And we would start a narrative or creative writing unit,
I would talk to the kids about starting their story
in the middle instead of the beginning

I had this one little boy who said that he took a plane
ride to visit his abuelita in a town in Mexico
I asked him what was the first thing he remembered,
and he said the smell in her kitchen
I suggested to start his story from that space and time
I saw him take off with his storytelling

I try to live in the present moment
I can see the forest for the trees
I can see what it was all for

I can feel the love in my heart and the

joy of experiencing my life

I could've missed it all

I have a friend who says you're right on time

I like that, not too slow, not too fast

right on time

Oprah

My twin girls were babies

I remember that first afternoon

Shangri-La

long naps

I was sitting on the couch and smoking my cigarettes,

Enjoying my Bartell and James wine cooler

only at nap time I told myself

Turned on the television

So much applause

A new talk show host Oprah Winfrey

3 PM channel 7

I was hooked from day one

I remember thinking this is perfect

I watch Oprah and unwind

so many problems solved

Mama Mommy Mom

I don't think it's a coincidence that my

children call me different names

I am different to each one of them just as they are to me

the tender moments, and hard talks

The tender moments

the hard talks

followed by a lifetime of joy

Sadie Sadie

Funny Girl was a huge part of my adolescence

I saw the musical recently

I was singing every song

I held my breath when the character

Nicky Arnstein came out

Flashy and wealthy- that was my standard for a man

Fanny Brice was my role model for a woman

not necessarily very pretty, but so lucky

she found a good man and fell in love

she got married and he would take care of her

Sadie, Sadie married lady

Printed in the United States
by Baker & Taylor Publisher Services